RELATIONSHIPS

LYNN PENSON

Copyright © CWR 2007

Published 2007 by CWR, Waverley Abbey House, Waverley Lane, Farnham, Surrey GU9 8EP, UK.

Registered Charity No. 294387. Registered Limited Company No. 1990308.

The right of Lynn Penson to be identified as the author of this work has been asserted by her in accordance with the Copyright, Designs and Patents Act 1988 sections 77 and 78.

See www.cwr.org.uk for list of National Distributors.

Unless otherwise indicated, all Scripture references are from the Holy Bible: New International Version (NIV), copyright © 1973, 1978, 1984 by the International Bible Society.

Concept development, editing, design and production by CWR

Printed in England by Bishops Printers

ISBN: 978-1-85345-447-9

CONTENTS

INTRODUCTION

As we open our Bibles, we are brought face to face with our theme of relationship in the very first phrase: 'In the beginning God …'. Genesis 1:1 introduces us immediately to a relational God, as the word translated as God comes from the plural 'Elohim'. Coming from the context of a rigorously monotheistic belief this may at first sight appear contradictory or at least a little strange. We hear loud and clear 'I am the LORD your God … you shall have no other gods before me' (Exod. 20:3), 'Hear O Israel: The LORD our God is one LORD' (Deut. 6:4). The uniqueness and oneness of God is both taught and assumed throughout the Old Testament Scriptures. Yet we have the plural Elohim in Genesis 1:1 and we read 'Let us make man in our image' (Gen. 1:26), 'Let us go down …' (Gen. 11:7), 'Who will go for us?' (Isa. 6:8). So, we encounter the Godhead who embodies relationship within His very being.

What has all this got to do with our twenty-first-century lives? We live in an age where relationships have become very complex. Those we would have treated with awe in a previous generation are now on first name terms with us. The once simple task of drawing a family tree for children is now often too complicated to attempt in the classroom. Social networking websites like 'My Space' have replaced former conventional ways of introducing yourself to other people. We live in a 'me' generation. Yet people long for meaningful relationships and it is meaningful relationship that we see portrayed in the Godhead and in His creative plan.

The aim of this *Life Issues* study guide is not to theorise about God but to look at what He reveals about Himself, and His plan in creating us. In this way, we understand how we can better relate to our boss, our children, our colleagues, our church family and the many other groups and individuals we interact with day by day. The studies aim to be very practical whilst being rooted in biblical truths. We trust that as you work through them you will find them informative, constructive and fun!

◎ Using the Material

This guide is designed to be used in a group study setting, though an individual can use it by adapting the group work as appropriate. Each group will handle the material differently but here are a few suggestions to help you get the most out of it:

- The studies will work more effectively if each person is encouraged to read through the material before coming together to discuss it.
- It might be helpful for each person to use a notebook to jot down answers, thoughts and reflections both during the session and between times together, although there is space to write in this book.
- At the end of each section are reflections, partly to round off the discussion but also with suggestions which some may want to use as a way of continuing to think about the subject between meeting together.
- A flip chart or large sheets of paper (plain wallpaper is a good alternative) and marker pens will be very useful to jot down ideas that come from the discussion.
- It would be helpful for the leader/facilitator to be familiar with the questions and activities in order to adapt them to the specific needs of the group.
- Most importantly, this study guide is about relationships and will be best used when group members feel comfortable and secure with each other. It is important that people feel they can be honest without being judged, and that they are assured of confidentiality.
- At the end of each session it would be good to spend time as a group reflecting on the positive aspects of relationship with God and with others that have been highlighted. Also, try to have a praise and prayer time to thank God for the relationships enjoyed by the group; for His relationship with us; and to pray about areas of relationship where we need God's help in moving forward.
- Enjoy and have some fun!

THE SOURCE OF RELATIONSHIPS

◎ Chill out

Everyone in the group should write down on a small piece of paper one thing about themselves that others in the group do not know. Fold the pieces of paper in half and put them in a pile; shuffle them and each person should take out one. Read each in turn and try to guess who wrote each description.

◎ Think through

Choose one or both of the following suggestions to start thinking together about the topic of relationships.

- *We are surrounded by relationships and these differ greatly: from those where we feel really comfortable and close, to those that are mere acquaintances. Discuss what the word 'relationship' means to you and write down the different levels of relationships you have. Try to identify the distinct features of these different relationships and compare them.*
- *What would your idea of a perfect relationship be? Write your own 'thought shower' and then compare your ideas with others in your group. There is space to write on the next page.*

◎ Think on

Today's society seems to be hovering on an uncertain brink. Do we go the way of the individual or of community? A shift in thinking (that has its roots in the seventeenth century) brought a change from a time when community took priority over the individual[1] to rampant individualism[2], where each person pursues their own happiness, irrespective of anyone else. The result is a 'me generation' rather than an 'us generation'. This way of thinking is now being challenged as we see its disastrous effect on society. It is particularly important that the Church takes this seriously and becomes a driving force in rebuilding communities. Why is it so important that the Church be involved in this? It is because relationship, and hence community, lies at the very centre of who God is and what His plan for creation was about. God lives in relationship Himself and His intention was that created humanity should reflect this aspect of His being and also live in relationship. Individualism is not a way of life supported by the teaching of the Bible.

Consider the Trinity: Father, Son and Holy Spirit. As noted in the Introduction, we have a remarkable picture of relationship as we see the One True God as Trinity. Larry Crabb writes,

> If one believes that God exists as three persons, who are distinct enough to actually relate to one another then it becomes clear somehow that the final nature of things is wrapped up in the idea of relationship ... God is a personal being who exists eternally in a relationship among persons. He is His own community.[3]

And so, as we explore Scripture, we discover one God who is a Trinity of Persons each living in perfect relationship to the others; portraying a mutuality of giving and receiving, and displaying loving creativity in action.

- *Can you begin to imagine what it would mean to exist within a trinity of persons co-existing in perfect harmony? What sort of things would characterise it? What would be missing?*

Here then is the Trinity, living in perfect harmony. Yet this relational energy does not remain within the Godhead but is partly directed outwards – firstly in the act of creation, and then as God engages with the world to sustain, redeem and bring all things to completion. All of this is the result of the unselfish, giving nature of God.[4]

An important part of God's phenomenal creative act was to make humankind in His image. Much has been written about what this means. One way of understanding it is that God has made us in such a way that, deep down, we want to live in relationships that reflect the harmonious internal communion present within God.

When God said, 'It is not good for the man to be alone. I will make a helper suitable for him' (Gen. 2:18), He had far more in mind than marriage. As Selwyn Hughes commented, just as relationship is an integral part of the Trinity, so it is an integral part of what it means to be human. When God called Abraham, He promised him descendants as numerous as the stars and grains of sand. Moses was promised that God would make a great nation out of those he was leading from Egypt. God's call, then, was not just personal and individual, but corporate.

When Jesus began His work of teaching, He called around Him a group of men to be part of that work and, as He travelled, His calling to people was to follow Him and become part of the kingdom of God. Here again, we see this theme of calling people not into an individualised faith but into a community based on relationship.

- *Read Ecclesiastes 4:7–12. Here is a very practical way of looking at some of the benefits of relationships. Write down what you find in this passage and go on to add extra reasons why you think that 'two are better than one'.*
- *Look up John 15:9,11; 1 Corinthians 1:3; 2 Corinthians 13:14. These verses mention five characteristics of God that are passed on to us. We hear of them often. Consider each one and what it actually means for you.*
- *In what ways does God's 'unselfish, giving nature' show in His actions towards us? Look at the following verses to get you started: Romans 5:8, Ephesians 1:7, 2:7–8, 1 John 4:9–10.*

- *As bearers of God's image, what is our responsibility in reflecting the unselfish, giving nature of God?*
  What actions are required in order that we may reflect God's giving nature?
  Look up the following verses to get you started: Matthew 18:33, Colossians 3:13, Hebrews 12:14, 1 John 4:7.
- *Read Romans 12:9–18. On a piece of paper, make two lists of the advice given by Paul to the Romans about a) what should be avoided, and b) what should be put into practice, in relating to others. Spend a few moments on each, considering what impact it would make if we followed that advice. Which do you find easiest in this list and which most challenging? What can you apply immediately to your life situation?*

XTRA

- *Try to develop a pictorial representation showing: God's attributes, how they are shown in the life of Jesus, how they are poured into us, and how we go on to impact the world.*

One of the characteristics of the Godhead referred to is 'peace'. We sometimes associate peace with silence or quiet and it is used in that way at times in the Bible. However, the more widely used word in the New Testament is the Greek word *'eirene'* which actually has the meaning of 'unity' or 'concord'. This is not the peace that is achieved when we retreat to some quiet spot by ourselves. If *eirene* is about unity then it involves more than one person; it is not about me in isolation but about me in relationship with others. This peace is rooted in the Trinity: Father, Son and Holy Spirit living in perfect harmony. God's desire is that, firstly, we live in peace with Him, and this is achieved through

Christ (Eph. 2:13–14). Secondly, God wants us to live in peace with one another. If we, as communities of believers, want to reflect God then we must reflect the unity of the Trinity. In other words, we should pursue relationships with each other which show wholeness and unity.

What wonderful churches, families, communities and friendships we would have if our relationships were all based on being in unity or agreement with one another. Sadly, this is not always a true picture, just as was the case in the first-century Church. The authors of the New Testament letters often plead for people to live together in harmony. Paul pleads with Euodia and Syntyche – two women who have been involved in Paul's ministry – 'to agree with each other in the Lord' (Phil. 4:2). The reality is that disharmony always has been and always will be evident. Therefore the challenge remains, as true now as in the Early Church, to 'pursue peace'. It is a challenge well worth rising to meet.

Understanding how we naturally react to conflict can be very helpful as we work towards resolving a lack of harmony.

● *How do you react in a conflict? Do you identify with any of the following?*

- Prickly hedgehog – 'Don't come near me!'
- Head-in-the-sand ostrich – 'It will all blow over if I keep my head down.'
- Timid mouse – 'If I give in there won't be a problem.'
- Stubborn mule – 'I won't give in.'
- Attacking rhino – Head down and charge: 'You are so stupid', 'You will not ...'
- Unforgetting elephant – 'I won't forget', 'I remember when ...'
- Blind bat – Not even noticing there is a problem.

Jesus said, 'Blessed are the peacemakers' (Matt. 5:9). Are we able to put aside our natural way of responding to problems and be committed to working towards resolving them in the most appropriate way? If we do so, we are working towards being peacemakers. Paul writes that we should bear with each other in love and 'Make every effort to keep the unity of the Spirit through the bond of peace' (Eph. 4:3). Alongside this, we need to remember that to disagree is not always wrong or unhelpful – we have different ideas and ways of doing things because we are made to be different. The question is not 'do we disagree?' but 'how do we deal with that disagreement?' Our aim is unity, not uniformity.

- *Disagreements have so many different causes. Sometimes theological issues cause problems, but so often it is other matters. What sorts of things create disharmony and conflict in your life with others? (Look at what caused a problem at Corinth, in 1 Corinthians 14:20.)*
- *Look up the following verses and note what they say about peace: Romans 14:19, Colossians 3:15, 1 Peter 3:11. You may want to add others.*
  Discuss practical suggestions of how to 'pursue peace'. What difference would it make to our relationships if we did this in our home, church, work?

There may be aspects of this study that you find hard to live up to. Don't see them as a burden but rather as an invitation to form relationships that are good, wholesome and that start with what God lavishly gives to us.

◎ Reflection

Reflect on the positive aspects of your relationship with God, within your group and with others. This could lead to a time of praise and prayer together.

As you go about your day-to-day interactions this week, be aware of leaving a sense of peace behind you. What elements of this study will make a difference in how you get along with other people?

LOVING OTHERS

◎ Chill out
What is the kindest act that you can remember seeing or hearing about or that you have experienced personally? Why did it impact you so much?

◎ Think back
Think back to times you have spent with people over the past week. How do you think others have felt after spending time with you? Would they see the experience as positive or negative? Have you left them feeling at peace with you and with themselves wherever possible?

◎ Think through
- *Think of a particular relationship that was, or is, especially good. What is it that defines its positive impact on you?*

◎ Think on
The year 1990 was a watershed in my spiritual life and growth. Whilst on a course at Waverley Abbey, I was challenged as Selwyn Hughes spoke to us about finding our deep longings for security, self-worth and significance met in God rather than from our own resources. As he spoke, I knew this was to be a turning-point in my life, directing me to God, and away from other potential sources. My relationship with God took on a whole new dimension

as I learned to turn to and depend on Him for those needs. He is the one who truly meets our deepest longings.

A little while after this, I was asked to lecture on 'Making families that work', and later was involved in leading marriage enrichment weekends for Bible college students, along with my husband. In doing these, I began to see a pattern that has become an integral part of my belief system. I had already discovered that significance, self-worth and security are what we long for and they need to be found in God first; if we look elsewhere in the first instance, we will certainly face disappointment at some time. However, the way that God relates to me, meeting my deepest needs, is surely a wonderful blueprint for my relationships with others. For me as a wife, mother, friend, colleague, mentor, lecturer and teacher, I need to be pouring security, significance and self-worth into those relationships; and of course the best relationships I have are when that is reciprocated. I believe that, if we could take hold of this 'blueprint' for relationships, we would see transformed friendships, families, churches and communities.

We are going to look at these areas over the next three sessions. In doing so, we need to be aware that they do not divide up into neat packages. There is much that overlaps and each aspect has an effect on the others. Also, the examples used to illustrate each point could easily be seen as interchangeable. They are all a sign of love. If I love someone in the way that God loves me, I accept them unconditionally and I want to affirm their value and their significance. Of course our relationships are on many different levels but the principle can still stand.

It is helpful to consider what it means to feel fully secure in our relationship with God, and with other people, in order to work out ways of reflecting that security onto others. We are secure when we feel accepted and loved unconditionally. If any relationship is fully secure, that gives us peace, takes away the fear of rejection and it allows us to feel safe to fail. We may not enjoy failure, but can feel secure in the knowledge that failure will not make the other person think less of us or adversely affect our relationship. If we can pass on that sense of security to others, we will be passing on something of what God has given us and it will be a strong foundation for any sort of friendship.

A reality check tells us that there are times when this is going to be difficult! There may be some 'types' of people that we struggle with as our inbuilt prejudices kick in. We may react negatively to some personalities or to certain social or cultural backgrounds. There may be individuals who have caused such pain that love and acceptance do not seem to be an option. It may be that there are forgiveness issues to work through.

Our relationships are going to be on many different levels and we cannot, and should not, try to relate to everyone equally. However, giving and receiving unconditional love and acceptance will profoundly impact both close friendships and occasional encounters.

As we work through these areas, we need to remember that love, in this context, is not about emotion. It is an aspect of the will, requiring action. It is about what we think and how we behave.

- *Read 1 John 3:1. Meditate on this verse by taking a word or phrase at a time, savouring each part of it. Then look at it again as a complete verse. Share your thoughts.*

XTRA
- *As a group, think together about inbuilt prejudices and dislikes. Where do those come from and how might we learn to overcome the instincts that might hinder us from loving some people or groups?*
- *Discuss ways of showing unconditional love and acceptance to others. You may like to reflect on times when you have been on the receiving end and how you felt as a result.*

Unconditional love requires us to forgive. We are also required to look honestly at ourselves, recognising that we have not always got it right. We are going to consider some ways in which we can practically demonstrate our genuine love and acceptance of others but, in doing so, must remember that these acts do not define love, they simply add colour to it, helping us to demonstrate it to others.

By words
How many of you remember the ditty 'Sticks and stones may break my bones but words will never harm me'? How untrue! Words have power for bad as well as good. By carefully choosing words to show love and acceptance we can ensure that the recipient appreciates the love that we are trying to convey – Proverbs 25:11 tells us that 'A word aptly spoken is like apples of gold in settings of silver'. Remember that timing can play a part and that words are not only spoken but also written.

XTRA

- *Words have great power to do harm, but equally, great power to do good. Look for examples in Proverbs 15:1–4 and James 3:3–12.*
- *What examples of words spoken, to good and bad effect, have you experienced recently? How did you feel as a result?*
- *When might silence be of greater benefit than words?*

Personal Action

Make a commitment to write, phone or speak to someone in the next day or so, with words to encourage or affirm them.

By action

Nobody could ever suggest that Jesus was a man of words but not of action. Whether providing food for hungry people, health to the sick, wine for the wedding feast, water for tired and dusty feet or death for our life, Jesus was the true 'Action Man'; He shows us the importance of actions in communicating love and acceptance. The New Testament has a great deal to say about this. One example is found in Galatians 5:13: 'Serve one another in love.'

- *Read John 13:3–17 or 21:4–13. Put yourself in the place of a disciple. Think about how the disciple might have been feeling in the moments leading up to this incident, about Jesus' actions and the possible impact on the disciple's relationship with Jesus. Take time to feed back thoughts.*
- *Think of a time when you were on the receiving end of an act of kindness. How did you feel about it?*
- *How do acts of kindness and service impact a relationship?*

Personal Action

Think of two 'small' acts of kindness or service and two 'large' ones which you could carry out at home, church or in the community. Commit to do them in your chosen time frame.

Group Action

As a group you might consider changing one of your study evenings to an event where you could get involved in helping to meet a need within your group, church or community. Fun and food often go well with such projects!

By touch

This can be a difficult area in today's climate of fear and protection. However it is a powerful tool in our love kit box.

Many years ago, an experiment at the maternity unit in Bellevue Hospital in New York showed that the mortality rate for infants under one year old fell from 35% to less than 10% if the babies were picked up, carried around and 'mothered' several times a day. Similar findings have been noted in Eastern Europe orphanages. If the lack of touch contributes to physical death, might it also cause death to relationships?

- *Why is touch so important? In your group, discuss this issue. We need to be very aware of the concerns of inappropriate touch and how some people who have been abused may be very cautious, whilst others crave human touch and warmth.*

XTRA
- *'Greet one another with a holy kiss' (2 Cor. 13:12). Bearing in mind both the positive and negative impacts of physical touch, consider how you would want to interpret and apply this verse both within your group and beyond.*

By our presence

Presence is a delicious word ... Nothing else can take the place of presence, not gifts, nor telephone calls, not pictures, not mementos, nothing ... When we are ill, we don't need soothing words nearly as much as we need loved ones to be present. What makes shared life – games, walks, concerts, outings and a myriad of other things – so pleasurable? Presence.[5]

Do you identify with the above quote? If we are to have strong relationships with each other we need to spend time together. How we spend that time is vitally important and will, of course, be different for different relationships.

We have a very powerful picture of the importance of presence in Jesus' promise to send the Holy Spirit to come and indwell each believer, and also when He says, 'I am with you always' (Matt. 28:20).

Group Action
Have some fun planning an activity to do together and book a date for it.

◎ Reflection

Look back over this study and pick out one particular point that you would like to take on board this week.

As you live out your life this week you may wish to reflect on the opportunities you have had to show you care through speech, the written word and kind actions, and how you have felt when others have blessed you in these ways.

APPRECIATING OTHERS

◎ Chill out

Hand around a bowl of chocolates and sweets which include a variety of shapes, types, fillings, wrappings etc. Each person should choose one that says something about them, not just a favourite. Having explained its significance to the group, you could 'trade' with others for your favourite!

OR

'If I were a toy I would be …' Each person thinks about a toy that describes a facet of their personality or how they feel at this time, and shares their thoughts with the group.

◎ Think back

Think back to the topics discussed in the last session. Each person should give one example of a time since then when they were on both the giving and then the receiving end of one of those ways of showing love to others.

◎ Think through

- *What is it that you most appreciate and enjoy in other people? What is it that most annoys or frustrates you in others?*

◎ Think on

In the last session, we looked at how we find our security in God and ways in which we could pass that great gift on to others. In this study, the focus is on the area of 'value'.

A key to showing that we value other people is that we appreciate them, not just for what they are good at, or for their achievements, but simply for who they are. Paul writes, 'For we are God's workmanship' (Eph. 2:10). The word used for workmanship is the Greek word *'poeme'* which means a creative work, as opposed to *'erga'* which means labour or daily grind; *The Message* translates *poeme* as 'masterpiece'. This shows us something of God's view of us as His creation. Just as masterpieces come in all sizes, styles, colours and subjects but share one thing in common – they are all valuable – so we are all different but each of great worth to God. What a wonderful metaphor.

- *Each person in the group should look up one of the following references about how God values us, and explain it to the group: Isaiah 43:1, 1 Corinthians 6:19–20, Ephesians 2:6–7.*
- *In Romans 12:10 we read 'Honour one another' and in 1 Peter 2:17, 'Show proper respect to everyone'. Discuss how you would put those phrases into practice, giving specific examples.*

◎ Listening

God has clearly shown us how much He values us, in the enormous price paid for us through the sacrifice of Jesus. However, that is not the end of it. God continues to reveal how important we are to Him, communicating with us and listening to us.

A major contributing factor to feeling valued is to be heard and listened to. We may not find ourselves in a position to lay down our lives for someone else as Jesus did, but we can become better listeners, and in this way, impart value to others.

Listening plays an important role in the Scriptures. As we read the accounts of great men and women of the Bible, we find them in relationships where God not only spoke to them but also listened to them. God listened to the fears of Moses, Jeremiah and Samuel. He listened to the cries and groans of the Hebrew slaves in Egypt. Anne Long writes:

Father, Son and Holy Spirit are in constant listening communion with each other (John 16:13ff) ... [God] tells the world to listen to His son (Matthew 17:5). Jesus' mission was a constant rhythm of turning in obedient listening to His Father (John 8:28) then turning with compassion to listen to people, not only to their words but into the depths of their being (John 2:25; Luke 7:39,40)'.[6]

James encourages us to 'be quick to listen, slow to speak ...' (James 1:19). Listening does not necessarily come naturally, but it is one of the most profound ways of showing someone that you take them seriously and value their opinions. Listening requires more than simply hearing the words. It involves taking note of 'the bass line' and working at understanding what is being said.

Hearing is basically to gain content or information for your own purposes. Listening is caring for and being empathetic towards the person who is talking. Hearing means that you are concerned about what is going on inside you during the conversation. Listening means that you are trying to understand the feelings of the other person and are listening for [their] sake.[7]

We can listen in a number of ways: out of pity, out of obligation or 'niceness', inquisitively, as if not present, as a way of finding out facts which we can use for our own purposes, ready to leap in with our solutions, or we can listen in such a way that we are ready to give support, understanding and reassurance – 'listening for their sake'.

● *Divide into pairs. One person from each pair takes two minutes to relate a positive experience; it could be from childhood or more recently. The other person is to listen carefully. At the end of the two minutes the 'speaker' should say if they felt listened to. The listener then recounts the incident and the speaker reflects on the accuracy. Be prepared to be gracious about mistakes; even better, use humour!*

- *As a group, discuss together how you think good listening impacts relationships.*

We are told that the words we use account for only a small percentage of the effectiveness of our communication. Voice tone and body language account for the rest. That has implications for us as we listen. In order to truly understand, we need to be 'listening' to all those non-verbal as well as verbal signals.

XTRA

- *Look up Luke 7:36–50. What non-verbal messages did Jesus pick up on a) from the woman, b) from Simon, the Pharisee and host? In what ways did Jesus show this woman she was valued? What lessons can we learn from this about how we relate to others?*

◎ Understanding

As we have seen, understanding undergirds good listening but there may be other areas of understanding we can explore in order to be generous in our giving of value to others. It is so easy to fall into the trap of either feeling inadequate ourselves or making others feel inadequate, because we do not appreciate the differences inherent in how God made us.

- *Look at the eight categories below. Out of each pair, who do you most identify with? What strengths do you see in yourself as a result?*
  Discuss your findings with a partner and then as a group. Talk about how this can help you to understand and appreciate each other and what you can take into other relationships.

Active Annie is a real people person who is most excited when around people and is energised by active involvement in events. She has a wide range of acquaintances and friends and feels comfortable working in groups.

OR

Reflective Rita prefers fewer, more intense relationships, feels comfortable being alone and is energised and excited when involved with ideas, images and reactions that are part of her inner world.

Focused Freda looks for facts, tends to be good with detail, and is practical and accurate. She likes to feel her feet are well and truly on the ground.

OR

Variety Vera is more interested in things that are new and different. She enjoys ideas and creativity. She likes to dream.

Thinking Theo is able to make decisions objectively and is not so concerned about what others may want. He is able to analyse, spot inconsistencies, and rates truth higher than tact.

OR

Heartfelt Henry is much more concerned about what is best for the people involved when making decisions. He wants to maintain harmony and comes over as caring and tactful.

Decided Dennis likes to have a planned and orderly life where things are settled and organised, decisions made and life is under control. He tends to plan his work to avoid rushing just before deadlines.

OR

Spontaneous Sam prefers to live a flexible lifestyle, open to new experiences and information which means he tends to put off making decisions. He prefers play to work and often enjoys rushing just before deadlines.

It is so easy to impose our preferred way of living on others, expecting that what is important to us must be important to them. However, if we live in this way our relationships will be harmed as others will feel they are not valued for who they are. As we grow in our understanding of others we can appreciate and value them for who they are and for what they bring to our friendships.

- *Think of someone you work or live with who is quite different from you. As you read the descriptions above, which do you think best portrays their characteristics? Do they come under different descriptions from you?*
  How might these differences create frustrations?
  How might their differences complement you?
  How might you be able to value and enjoy those differences more as you gain greater understanding of them?

A CREATIVE XTRA

- *Look back to what was said about Ephesians 2:10 ('Think on' section above). On a sheet of A4 plain paper, create an 'art gallery' under the heading of 'God's Masterpieces'. You could use either pictures or words to illustrate what you see in other people with whom you have a relationship.*

Reflections

Reflect on the wonderful diversity found among the people you know and how the friendships you have add 'colour' to your life. You may like to choose a song to listen to, such as Stuart Townend's song 'Before the Throne of God Above', the words of which are a profound reminder of our value to God – I have 'engraved you on the palms of my hands' (Isa. 49:16).

As you go through this week, think about positive ways in which you can show that you value the people you have a relationship with, whether at home, work or church.

AFFIRMING OTHERS

◎ Chill out

If you could be someone else, who would you choose to be?

◎ Think back

Looking back over this week, do you feel that you have been listened to and are you aware of having listened at a deep level to others?

◎ Think through

- *Think about the personalities in the media at the moment. How would you rate the value of their contribution to society?*

◎ Think on

Alongside the need to feel that we are accepted and valued for who we are, is the need to feel that we can make a valuable contribution to life; that is, having a sense of significance. Without it we live under the cloud of believing we are incompetent, with no sense of purpose and meaning. If this is a deep longing in us, it needs to be met firstly in God, but it is also part of the equation for good relationship building.

Scripture suggests that we are far from incompetent. God has plans for us (Jer. 29:11) and He has good works prepared for us to do (Eph. 2:10). When Paul writes to the church in Corinth he says, 'God ... has committed to us the message of reconciliation. We are therefore Christ's ambassadors, as though God were making his appeal through us' (2 Cor. 5:19–20). How amazingly significant that is! Reconciliation – the great work of Christ as He made a way for us to be brought back into relationship with God through His death – has now been passed on to us; we are entrusted with this powerful task as Christ's ambassadors or representatives.

For the past year, I have worked with the parent and toddler group at my church. At times I have reflected on the contrast between teaching theology to degree-level students (as I have done in the past) and ripping up tissue paper to create collage butterflies. I absolutely believe that both are equally significant in fulfilling the calling to be God's ambassador; passing on the 'message of reconciliation'.

- *In what ways do you see yourself as being God's ambassador to others? How do you feel about being entrusted with this 'message of reconciliation'?*

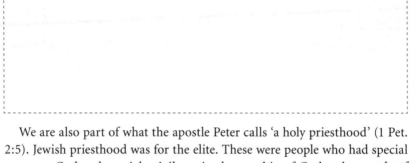

We are also part of what the apostle Peter calls 'a holy priesthood' (1 Pet. 2:5). Jewish priesthood was for the elite. These were people who had special access to God and special privileges in the worship of God – the people of Israel relied on them as their representatives to God. We no longer need an intermediary: we are told we can come directly to God. Each person within our small group, our church and the worldwide Church is a holy priest. This gives us significance as individuals, and we should see our fellow believers as significant too.

How does all of this impact on how we relate to others in our church, our family, at work and elsewhere? Firstly we'll consider what the Bible teaches us about how we relate within the community of the Church, and then we'll think about how we also put those principles into action in our relationships outside the Church.

The epistles provide us with some wonderful pictures to help our understanding, and some excellent advice on how to translate this understanding into action. One of those pictures is found in 1 Peter 2:4–5: we are 'living stones being built into a spiritual house', a temple. See also Ephesians 2:19–22.

As people, we come with our different personalities, skills, gifts, preferences. Some of us are creative, others very practical; some visionary, others better at the nitty gritty; some good with children, some with technology; some with a balance sheet, others with a teapot and box of tissues. Each one of us is significant. We are all living stones, each with our different strengths, abilities and talents, all coming together, to build a 'spiritual house' – the vast house of God. What a wonderful picture we have of each of us with our different personalities, skills and experience being built together into this growing, sacred structure where God can be honoured.

A similar picture is painted in 1 Corinthians 12:12–27 using the illustration of the body. Both these pictures – of the body and the temple – have a powerful way of affirming our value and significance, and that of others. After all, the body needs the foot as much as the eye, and the house needs each part of the structure in order to remain suitable for the purpose for which it was built. There is no place here for us to feel inferior, nor to feel superior, which equally means that there is no place for us to see others as inferior or superior. We all have significance in the kingdom of God.

So how do we help others feel significant, whether friends, family or co-workers? I offer the following suggestions:

1) We recognise their talents and strengths.
2) We value and appreciate their abilities, encouraging and supporting them.
3) We celebrate their success.

In the account following the slaying of Goliath and other victories in battle (1 Sam. 18) we see two very different responses to David's success. Saul wanted David to remain with him but soon became jealous and angry, whereas Jonathan became a loyal and supportive friend. When we see success in others, how do we respond? Do we feel threatened by their ability or do we recognise and support their talent and so enable them to become confident and grow to reach their potential?

- *Each person should take a sheet of paper, write their name at the bottom and pass it to the next person. Everybody in turn writes a comment about the skills or talents they identify in the one whose name is written, folds over their writing and passes it on until it gets back to the named person, who can then read what has been written by the group.*

I would say that I do not have any artistic creativity in my make-up. However, I offered to do a craft activity one day with the parent and toddler group and before long I was awarded the grand title of Head of Creative Activities, much to the amusement of my family, friends, and me in particular! How could I do this? It was due to the incredible encouragement of the leader of the group who is very arty but could still value my simple efforts with the toddlers. I now plan with excitement and enjoy my creative sessions. I have discovered that the greatest asset you can have for this role is a good sense of humour, which in my case makes up for lack of artistic expertise!

As we speak words of encouragement and affirmation to others, we enable them to achieve their potential. We also deepen our friendships with this spirit of generosity.

- *Can you identify a time when someone recognised a gift or ability in you, when you were feeling uncertain about it?*
- *Read 1 Corinthians 12:12–26. (See also Ephesians 4:16.)*
  a) *What do verses 12–21 tell us about the value of each part of the body?*
  b) *Read verses 23–24. In what ways can this be put into practice and how does that relate to you as a group of people in your church? How should this affect the way you view and value one another?*
  c) *What does verse 26 say about how we respond to the joys and sorrows of others?*
  d) *Think of some practical ways of responding to those who are suffering. Try to be creative in your ideas.*
  e) *Think of some practical ways of rejoicing with others.*
  f) *Make a commitment to a) do something for someone you know who is struggling at the moment, b) celebrate with someone who has done something well.*
- *So far, we have been looking particularly at relationships within the community of believers. In what ways can these principles also be reflected in relationships at work, in the family and elsewhere?*

WEEK FOUR: AFFIRMING OTHERS

Personal action

Make a list of four or five people you encounter in your day-to-day life, eg your boss, colleague, a family member or someone you enjoy a hobby with. What are they really good at doing? Make a point of letting them know over the next week or so.

One of the first acts of Jesus after His baptism and temptation was to call together a group of people – His disciples. We see that Jesus did not 'go it alone' but rather He chose to have others around Him. He worked with, and through, what we might consider a rather motley group of men. Think of the very different backgrounds and personalities of the disciples. William Barclay writes, 'if Simon the Zealot had met Matthew anywhere else than in the company of Jesus, he would have stuck a dagger in him'.[8] Yet Jesus called each one of them, firstly to be with Him and then to give them the task to go out and preach with authority. This is a vivid picture of acceptance, value and significance being poured into His relationship with them.

It is often easier to work with people who are similar to us, who have the same way of doing things, the same value system, and the same priorities. But that is not necessarily the best way to get a good job done and it is certainly not what Jesus elected to do. Good relationships are forged when we recognise and value the differences there are between us, work with them and enjoy them.

Reflection

Spend some time reflecting on the example Jesus gave us in the way He related to people, and then think of the people you relate to, with all their different values, abilities, temperaments and backgrounds. Thank God for them and for the people He has brought into your life to encourage and support you.

Pray that you can be generous in the way you relate to others, whether they are people that you easily get along with or that you struggle with. Pray that your relationships will be real, positive and enjoyable.

I have adapted some words from Colossians 2:2–3 as my prayer for you as you complete this study:

I pray that you will be encouraged in heart and united in love, that you may have the full riches of complete understanding, and above all that you may know Christ, in whom are all the treasures of wisdom and knowledge. Amen.

Notes

[1] David Bosch, *Transforming Mission* (Mary Knoll, NY: Orbis Books USA, 1992) p.267.

[2] Ibid., p.273.

[3] Larry Crabb, quoted in Selwyn Hughes, *Christ Empowered Living* (Farnham: CWR, 2001) p.19.

[4] Millard Erickson, *Christian Theology* (London: Marshall Pickering, 1986).

[5] Gordon Fee Paul, *The Spirit and the People of God* (London: Hodder and Stoughton, 1997).

[6] Anne Long, *Listening* (London: Daybreak, 1990).

[7] Norman H. Wright, *More Communication Keys for Your Marriage* (Ventura, Ca: Regal Books, 1995).

[8] William Barclay, *Gospel of Matthew Vol 1* in *The Daily Study Bible* series (Edinburgh: St. Andrew Press, 1978)

OTHER RESOURCES FROM CWR...

Life Issues for Homegroups: Forgiveness

This group study by Ron Kallmier is written in the firm belief that forgiveness is an important element of personal wellbeing. It is designed to help us explore important biblical teaching on the subject – and to address the practical matters involved in both forgiving and being forgiven.

£2.99
ISBN: 978-1-85345-446-2

We currently have seven daily dated Bible reading notes. These aim to encourage people of all ages to meet with God regularly in His Word and to apply that Word to their everyday lives and relationships.

Every Day with Jesus - devotional readings for adults. ISSN: 0967-1889
Inspiring Women Every Day - for women. ISSN: 1478-050X
Lucas on Life Every Day - life-application notes. ISSN: 1744-0122
Cover to Cover Every Day - deeper biblical understanding. ISSN: 1744-0114
Mettle - for 14-18s. ISSN: 1747-1974
YP's - for 11-15s. ISSN: 1365-5841
Topz - for 7-11s. ISSN: 0967-1307

£2.25 each per bimonthly issue (except *Mettle*: £3.99 per four-month issue).

Get the benefit of Insight

The *Waverley Abbey Insight Series* gives practical and biblical explorations of common problems, valuable both for sufferers and for carers. These books, sourced from material first presented at Insight Days by CWR at Waverley Abbey House, offer clear insight, teaching and help on a growing range of subjects and issues.

Self-esteem: 978-1-85345-409-7
Eating Disorders: 978-1-85345-410-3
Stress: 978-1-85345-384-7

Bereavement: 978-1-85345-385-4
Anxiety: 978-1-85345-436-3
Anger: 978-1-85345-437-0

£7.50 each

Courses from CWR

We run a range of biblically-based training courses at our headquarters of Waverley Abbey House, Farnham, Surrey, England. These include courses on counselling and on life issues such as forgiveness.

For more details, call our Training Department on **+44 (0)1252 784700** or visit our website: **www.cwr.org.uk**

Prices correct at time of going to print.